Praise

"Kamstra embraces every encounter, believing they guide him to a higher plane of existence. As a result, his poems seek to answer the voice within all of us that has wondered 'why me' or 'when will things change' and provides an encouraging answer: We have the power to evolve into something greater when we view each life experience as a valuable gift and an opportunity to be reborn."
CATHERINE LoFRUMENTO-FOSTER, POET

"Bauke's poetry is all at once tender and surreal, bursting with a playful curiosity about the sensual lives of we humans. A poet to keep coming back to!"
BRENDAN BONSACK, POET, RADIO 3CR

"The micro format once again brings a big presence in a small package, and Bauke's razor wit shines through with ever increasing brightness. A beacon to give us guidance in the dark places that come and go."
TYLER SALZMAN, HISTORIAN

"Bauke Kamstra is a writer I have read for many years and whose words can, at times, make you feel that he knows you. Or you wish to know him, to reach out and touch him, except one does not wish to take their eyes off his writing. They are as film visuals and touch you in every sense of feeling, shape and form. Some will hold your mind with its gentle hand, while others shake your thoughts, shapeshifting each movement you feel within your own life, touching you with the thoughts of others you love, have loved, held and cherished."
CHEY LAINE, POET

About the Author

Residing in Nova Scotia, surrounded by big sea and small mountains, beauty is immediate. The sensuous allure of lovers, the kiss and the complex, eloquent tongue, brings beauty to passion, makes synapses sing, and the heart to love.

Volume 4

Passion Demands a Vocabulary of Desire

101 TWEETS TO INSPIRE YOUR FOLLOWERS

BAUKE KAMSTRA

Vine Leaves Press
Melbourne, Vic, Australia

Passion Demands a Vocabulary of Desire
101 Tweets to Inspire Your Followers
Volume IV
Copyright © 2020 Bauke Kamstra
All rights reserved.

Print Edition
ISBN: 978-1-925965-38-4
Published by Vine Leaves Press 2020
Melbourne, Victoria, Australia

No parts of this publication may be reproduced, stored in a retrieval system, or transmitted in any form or by any means, electronic, mechanical, photocopying, recording, or otherwise, without the prior written permission of the copyright owner.

This book is sold subject to the condition that it shall not, by way of trade or otherwise, be lent, resold, hired out, or otherwise circulated without the publisher's prior consent in any form of binding or cover other than that in which it is published and without a similar condition including this condition being imposed on the subsequent purchaser. Under no circumstances may any part of this book be photocopied for resale.

This is a work of fiction. Any similarity between the characters and situations within its pages and places or persons, living or dead, is unintentional and coincidental.

Cover design by Jessica Bell
Interior design by Amie McCracken

A catalogue record for this book is available from the National Library of Australia

About this Book

This is a book for savoring, for relishing, for sharing with the world. The ebook version comes as a gift with this book, and within the digital copy are links with each poem to share with your followers on Twitter. We want to change the world by injecting beauty and passion, and you can help us do that by sending these words out. Provoke conversation and bring some style and charm to your social media presence.

Please visit **bit.ly/volume-four-pyt** and use the password **passion1** to download your free copy of the ebook.

for Ellen

Volume 4

do it to me again
please

that thing with your hands.

Bauke Kamstra

it is ok
to be thirsty
for thought is a desert
& a flood of light

it is also a well.

Volume 4

for you are there
gathering softness
& I am there
verging on that softness
& when you open
I put my words in you
& you are mine.

Bauke Kamstra

the ear I never
listen with
is not immune to sound

though I find sounds
are sometimes made

within the skull.

you know when there is damage
& you think it is severe

but it is not

in this universe
we can remove our clothes at will
and take the consequence.

Bauke Kamstra

turn the distance
with a breaking branch
a rustle of leaves

you move through me
and never arrive.

how far can you go
when your heart
carries you backwards

doing nothing & you find
you are still parked.

Bauke Kamstra

a Russian moon seems different
you think
it's not a different moon

it's about
where you put your feet.

I wish I were thin
so thin
no
spectral
so I could drift through walls
or fly to the moon
or to you
just like a balloon.

Bauke Kamstra

just remember
this cage

is for your protection.

Volume 4

> all my fingers
> ache
> for your curves.

Bauke Kamstra

it is a three-cigarette day
but I'll leave you to imagine

if that's a lot
or not very much.

I've been around the world
yet there are countries
I will never visit

too many shadows.

Bauke Kamstra

it is not furniture
that makes a home & it seems

it is not you either.

gifted with colors
I cannot explain
I like that shirt on you

I like it off you too.

Bauke Kamstra

when do things start over
with a new person
inside this thing of people

so what do I do
just pick one?

emojis are becoming
self-aware viral infections

I'm not worried
I've a fist emoji
to protect me
& beat all the others.

Bauke Kamstra

sometimes we hurt ourselves most
by loving ourselves
over others.

I thought pain
would make me kind
but kindness hurts more.

being undone is not
as dramatic
as it sounds

e.g. the simple unclasp of a bra
so potentially perilous
but so statistically unlikely.

Volume 4

what with
the wide hips
swayed
air enough
for breath
the chant muffled
flesh
the moan inside
black
& fresh.

Bauke Kamstra

days when need disappears

when you rise
on my horizon
a small moon of desire
& listening

I hear you breathe.

the sweet shock
that is flesh
tiny hives when the air is cool

easily smoothed
by my touch
its blessing
its warmth.

Bauke Kamstra

passers by haggard
as discarded milk cartons

breathing the same
rancid breath

there is an honest rot beneath
every perfume.

a daisy gasp
shedding petals

the last is never
the one you want

falling deep
into a bucket of
raw brown sugar.

Bauke Kamstra

I've learned to rub my sticks
& crick the air
the way cicadas enhance
the sun

call me peter sans
church

I'll build a rock.

the man circling
a still child in his hands
limbs trailing

you know he burns
from his silhouette
but not enough

to make him a saint.

Bauke Kamstra

your horn is gigantic
against my ear

my own placement is more
appropriate

clouds stack over each other
making a city
of air.

who are you
to have called me
from sleeping in my sins

I embark
on a career
of breathing

holding you close.

Bauke Kamstra

each part
a fragment
of desire

the v goes both ways

the invite of spread feet
the apex
& the dive in.

your breath in my lungs
stolen
nothing of value
lunar light glints
on the gold tooth
in your mouth

red in this light.

Bauke Kamstra

having prepared to bleed
ship heaving through
final outriggers
of fog
I know the cannons are loaded
prepared to fire
I spread my arms wide.

Volume 4

all resonance
a song
or light
time
the space between molecules
my fingers
touching you.

Bauke Kamstra

you carry me in your teeth
wrapped in your furled tongue
laughing a breeze
fingering
the lifted pleats I trace
the circumference

my braille compass.

your flesh is my ink
your breath a muse
your soul the light that comes first
before others
the flower that will not fade
the song outlasting
the bird.

drop me in the sweat
the humid atmosphere
of vice

each desire has its own itch
its scaly patch of skin

drink in that venomous milk
a toxic breath
of sin.

I want to be inside
your knowledge

heads laid inside their pillows

nodding being into
a lick of ears

hold your white breath.

Bauke Kamstra

undress me in
this dark room
& find the
soul I've hidden
in small hours
& the wisps
of cloud &
smoke I breathe
out in this chill.

what was it
that made you forget life

your own ghost
frail whispers

induced to forswear
orgasm
uterine wastes

burned
at your request.

Bauke Kamstra

give me inches

strap my dick
to a bamboo board

(secrets of the ancients)

with a little effort
I can ensure
my manhood grows.

faith is in things
unseen
belief that my lover
loves
it is your air that I
breathe
minds know only
distance
but spirits merge.

Bauke Kamstra

you've used violence
to split my words
stacked like cordwood
ready to burn
scrap chips used
to take this to press

squeezing it that way
takes out the juice.

shall we rage like winter
giving up the ghost

snowing on the idea
of spring

a one last destructive
breath.

Bauke Kamstra

swallows are gone

thermometers prove
it isn't the cold

air quality
tests poor
but not fatal

I ought to mourn.

you do not hear
when I speak
gestures
unperceived

I've tried tapping stones
breathing in sync

I've not
reached you yet.

Bauke Kamstra

sticking my hands
in earth is not
that they sprout
but somehow extend
roots my ears
become vines
waving breezes
dropping fruit.

it is always snowing
the land is white
air is white
trees are white
houses all white
me too.

Bauke Kamstra

shadow shapes
unconsolidated fear

could not pilfer
enough breath
through mute
weak
shy
lips

why is it so hard
to kiss.

Volume 4

outside the cave
making fire

inside the cave
making marriage

prehistoric origins.

Bauke Kamstra

beyond the fence
a jagged step

a zombie-silent stranger
life stressed
bearing a child

broken into pain breath
a faltering smoke.

what voice I've left
hung on air
listening is not a preferred skill

my thumb rakes my ear
but still I cannot hear.

Bauke Kamstra

crunching a crust
of brown-dry
burn where the
shade prevents rain

yet another earth
shunned by clouds.

I've grown so
I can no longer
walk on air

being grounded
like a child
is a grown-up's choice

consequences go
then fade.

Bauke Kamstra

since you were lost
I cannot breathe

the garden has come up weeds

my voice has gone
into gray skies.

I may've been a latchkey kid
all those years

my memories are wax
but lighter
airborne

dispersed until I don't
remember them any more.

Bauke Kamstra

it is strange enough
in here

out there
where sirens define space

it is stranger.

a bump here
a pot there
I'm falling apart

but falling
is exactly
what I do

I would love
to fall into you.

Bauke Kamstra

we've barely touched space
it doesn't matter
we know the void

watched ourselves
cross the dark.

only ash is silent

except for the clatter
of burnt bone.

Bauke Kamstra

often breathless
but not poised
on exhilaration's brink

trachea a hawser docked

diaphragm muscle
a fist squeaked.

your face full of silent vows
no hint of which promise

whispered with that
breath like ash

effluvia blown
from the shell.

Bauke Kamstra

led by eyes lost
even if closed

I am found by silence.

words will follow you
but thoughts are lost back
at the end of the void

silence
is at the front.

Bauke Kamstra

so many darks
are sleepless

but not mine

unfolding like shadows
or flowers

living in silence.

colors unnamed
stressing air

wavelengths outside my eye

seconds
to measure your breath

frequencies
of your rising chest.

Bauke Kamstra

I've not gone
to the moon for you

though I've made the attempt

at some point
breathing loss

always forces me back.

covered by dark
but sure I want
something better

one can die
from a lack of love

as much as
too little oxygen.

Bauke Kamstra

you touched hands
yet it
might as well be
a kiss stretched
through air
our different
countries a good-bye
when we've
never met.

do not presume
to tell me

I am my own poetry.

a condensed book
consecrating that triangular
space

tells me all the science
I need

but does not tell me why
I need you.

bio-chemical awkwardness
binds us tight

no space exists
between us

a separation
as unthinkable
as a black hole

or its horizon.

I would save you
if I knew how

push
bad air
from your lungs

pump in fresh

knowing
that heart
never quits.

I raise you
above my head
& keep you there

like a feather
upon my breath

no interest accrues
on love
except mine.

Bauke Kamstra

my voice harsh
unforgiving
mired in earth

my spirit floats
a gentle breath carried
by the wind.

the lovers hard against stone
decapitated snake
a loose rope limp
at their feet

breathless
in its unravel.

Bauke Kamstra

I've thought with wings
in the way of crows
where everything is flight

my hands talk volumes
my heart
an eclectic silence.

was it only my body
which kept you?

you know how hot fails

perhaps that's why you left
pursuing a music
before it fades.

Bauke Kamstra

wisdom watches
as the axe falls

flinch the echo crack
or stones breaking
in the fire

numinous words rise only
in silence.

scarce-lit pictures
under grimed glass
untidy
undusted
as all the rest

I'm sure
you're in here
somewhere.

Bauke Kamstra

dragged behind
like a spider
or balloon
with only ordinary air

the gun
was left for dead
no
answering shots.

what is not said
is loudest & breaks
mythic barriers

a mad wringing
of hands

we leave behind
a beauty of silence.

Bauke Kamstra

bright strips ripped
off thought words

an expressive breath
as of a god

something in the way spring grows.

lux intoxicant
dreaming of space
the eyes of stars

a stylus
resolves into flesh

I will write myself down
upon you.

Bauke Kamstra

you cannot read
a mountain's light
(castrate as air)

no two fools agree
but wise men
don't know either.

an infinite wick
burnt at the ends
the flame is all life

ego is a glutton
a mutation of mind

watch how you pass
down its throat.

Bauke Kamstra

so little spirit
& nothing at all
of soul

the blade whirl
a chop of grief

perpetual churning
smothers the breath.

one lung was whittled down
to nothing
she has
one lung left
for her shaved whispered breath

knotted
& scratched.

Bauke Kamstra

too much noise
in the space
between us

I cannot sound you out

roads
have become walls

I can not find you.

strangeness of eyes
penetration

breaching etheric walls
& talking with stars

I breathe light
clear as birds
breathe flight.

Bauke Kamstra

having been broken
you hold breath
writing new lyrics your song
might transcend in
every way
but one.

Volume 4

I try to not smell anything
until I get close to you.

Bauke Kamstra

underwear so fine
so nearly transparent
hardly there

I know you wore them for me
to let me take them
to take you.

I say my own name
when I pray
sour-sweet

at least
I answer back.

Bauke Kamstra

walls disappear
when you forget them

mountains turn to air

that does not mean
they are not still there.

Volume 4

I have a calendar of names
a cluster of dates I can't find

maybe I ate them.

Bauke Kamstra

what is it about
back roads & dust
in summer

they save deposits
for my car.

every day gets longer
until they don't
& you begin to pray.
why do you think
you are silent

is it because you only
scream inside?

Bauke Kamstra

rage goes down
but its flames go up

this is what burns me.

longing is science
but measurements
record only heat

when I see you some
of these temperatures

rival the sun.

Bauke Kamstra

the line I drew
broke
& the bird I made
never flew.

I do not need your
boxer-rim
butt flash
plumber pic perspective
enlightening me

to my own human flaws.

Acknowledgements

I would like to thank Jessica Bell and the other hard-working people at Vine Leaves for bringing this book into the light.

Vine Leaves Press

Enjoyed this book?
Go to *vineleavespress.com* to find more.

Lightning Source UK Ltd.
Milton Keynes UK
UKHW030655231020
372100UK00006B/150